A Continuation of the Defence of the Remarks on Dr. Wells's Letters. In a Fifth and Sixth Letter to the Doctor. By James Peirce

A
Continuation
OF THE
DEFENCE
OF THE
REMARKS
ON
Dr. *WELLS's*
LETTERS.

In a Fifth and Sixth Letter to the Doctor.

By *JAMES PEIRCE.*

LONDON,
Printed by *J Humfreys,* for *John Lawrence*
at the Angel in the *Poultry.* 1707.

A Fifth Letter Addres'd to Dr. Wells, *in An*
fwer to his Two Letters, in reference to the Re
marks on his Letter to a Diffenting Parifhioner.

S I R,

I Have perus'd your Letter to my felf, and that at the End
to a Diffenting Parifhioner, in reference to the Remarks
in my Second Letter and do now return you my Thoughts
concerning them I ould have done it immediately, if
I had thought your Letters had contain'd any thing material in
the Controverfy, or difficult for a common Reader to fee
through, but finding it otherwife, I thought 'twould be time
enough to anfwer thefe, when you give me occafion for another Anfwer I fuppofe you will not be angry, that I judge
your unprov'd Affertions *of my falfe Arguing, falfe Interpretati-*
on, falfe Doctrine, and other difingenuous and foul Dealing, to be
only Words us'd to amufe your Reader, and to be a Trick and
Sham, which you think will be of Service in a Difpute When
you fhall have *fwell'd your Anfwer to a confiderable Bulk,* it 'tis
all like this fhort Specimen you have given us of it, I fhall e-
fteem it as demonftrative in Evidence and Proof of a triumphant
and total Victory, as a Difputant can defire What you have
faid hitherto is fo very trifling, that a little more of the fame
nature, will make me defpair of arguing with you, which I
mention, that I may engage you to writ with more Strength
and Evidence, and then the confident Boaflings and Triumphs,
which appear now with fo ill a Grace in your Writings, will
better become them I took your own Method, and anfwer'd
you in the Order you had fet things, and yet you are for a new
one. I could perhaps guefs the Reafon, if I were as free on
that Head as you are But, Sir, you fhall take what Method
you pleafe, and, provided you will but talk to the Purpofe, I
fhall be ready to attend you

You boaft in your Thefes concerning the Invalidity of Prefbyterian Ordination, which, you fee, I am ready to difcufs,
and have given you my Reafons why I think otherwife of them
than you do

And I fhall be as ready as you to debate the fecond Queftion you propofe, whether you or we are guilty of Schifm?

A 2   And

[4]

And I hope my Aims and Endeavours in clearing this Matter are as laudable as yours. I shall now confider what you fay in this Letter to me concerning fome Scraps you have pick'd out of my two firft Letters.

You fay, *Whereas I fet you forth in feveral Places, and particularly the firft and laft Paragraphs of my fecond Letter, as a moſt uncharitable Fellow* (but Fellow is not my word, 'tis your own tho' the Reader might fuſpect it to be mine, as 'tis Printed) *on account of the damning Sentences which you pafs on me and my Party. Could you but prevail with me to ufe Moderation, and with Coolnefs of Temper to confider of the Matter, you perfwade your felf, that I should quickly perceive that I fpeak very improperly, not to fay falfly, when I affirm you pafs damning Sentences upon us.*

Well, Sir, you have eafily gain'd this Point, and have prevail'd with me to ufe *Moderation, and Coolnefs of Temper*; but yet I can't perceive any thing of what you fay, becaufe I can't, how ever moderate *I am,* put out my own Eyes, or contradict the plain Teftimonies they give me in this Cafe. But you go on thus. *You can't but your felf own* (Letter 1ft, p 60.) *that any Sin, and confequently Schifm, is of it felf of a deftructive damning Nature. And this, I fuppofe, you own, (as well as I) becaufe the Scripture plainly declares fo much. Whence it follows, that either you, as well as I, pafs damning Sentences on Schifmaticks, or elfe, that 'tis neither you nor I, but in reality the Scripture, that paffe damning Sentences againft Schifmaticks, and what either you or do, when we fay that Schifmaticks are in a State of Damnation, can to ſuch amount to no more, than a Declaration of the damning Sentences paffed by the Scripture on Schifmaticks.*

Can any thing be more trifling and incoherent than this? Certainly if you had both a good Caufe, and Ability to manage it, you would not talk after this loofe rate. I own, *that any Sin, and fo Schifm, is of a deftructive damning Nature in it felf* that is, that it deferves Damnation, and without pardoning Grace, would infer it. But may I therefore fay, becaufe there is no Sin free from Sin, that all Men are in a State of Damnation? When we talk of Mens being *in a State of Damnation* we mean fomewhat more than their doing that which in it own nature deferves Damnation, *viz.* their being fuch, who have no Right by the Covenant of Grace to Pardon and Salvation but this Right a Man may have, notwithftanding feveral Sins which in their own Nature are deftructive. So that the Queftion here really comes to this, Whether, according to the Gofpel, it be certain, that a Man who believes in Chrift, and fincerely performs his whole Duty to God, as far as he knows using too all the means for the Knowledge of it, and yet, through miſtak miſtake in diſputable Matters not eſſential to Religion, is guil ty of Schiſm, is thereby excluded from all Benefits by the Covenant of Grace, and ſo in ſuch a Condition, that if he dies in it, he ſhall be certainly damn'd? This, I ſay, is falſe, and therefore, tho I own'd Schiſm in its own nature d mining, I deny'd that all Schiſmaticks are in a State of Damnation, more particularly expreſs'd my Charity tow ud your Piety, whom I judge to be guilty of that Sin. You add *This being ſo, it will follow (ſuppoſing I ſhould be miſtaken in the Accuſation, yet) the utmoſt I can be guilty of, in applying to the Diſſenters the damning Sentences paſs'd by the Scripture on Schiſmaticks, is only a bare Error of Judgment, and there is not the leaſt Ground for accuſing me of Uncharitableneſs.*

But, with your good leave, Sir, do not the Proteſtants on good Ground accuſe the Papiſts of *Uncharitableneſs,* for damning all out of their own Church, and yet notwithſtanding this, is an Error in their Judgments? And indeed your very Judgment (as well as theirs) is uncharitable; and that renders your Uncharitableneſs the more inveterate and deadly. And your very Judgment, as I have obſerv'd in my ſecond Letter, p. 32 is moſt injurious to thoſe Notions we are to form of God, and his Goodneſs from his Word. We don't accuſe you as uncharitable, becauſe you endeavour to convince Perſons of what you judge to be a Miſtake, but becauſe you ſo raſhly condemn your Neighbours, when they do not by their Infidelity or Diſobedience to the Laws of Chriſt, give you any ground for it. And therefore I ſhall here uſe the Words of Arch Biſhop *Tillotſon,* in his Sermon on 1 Cor. 3 15 " I grant that no Charity " teaches Men to ſee others damn'd, and not to tell them the " Danger of their Condition, But 'tis to be conſider'd, that " damning of Men is a very hard thing, and therefore whenc- " ver we do it, the Caſe muſt be wonderfully plain.

And therefore afterwards he ſays thus ; " And I do aſſure " you, I had much rather perſwade any one to be a good Man, " than to be of any Party or Denomination of Chriſtians what- " ſoever. For I doubt not but the Belief of the ancient Creed, " provided we entertain nothing that is deſtructive of it, to- " gether with a good Life, will certainly ſave a Man.

After I had allow'd that Schiſm is in it ſelf of a deſtructive damning nature, I added, *let we take not upon us to judge the Conformiſts Eternal State, as they, many of them, do very freely ours. We know they have a merciful God to deal with, who knows how to make Allowances for the Prejudices of Education, or the Byaſs, that the Vogue of the World, or Intereſt, do in ſome meaſure give to Men that are yet truly ſincere and upright. Upon this,*

A 3

this, tho it be not in the Letter you pretend to animadvert
on, you waite no lefs than three Pages, which, together with
the perfect Innocence, Charity and Truth of the Paſſage, will,
I doubt not, convince unprejudic'd Perſons, that you wanted
Matter for this Letter, and were more concern'd to ſay ſome
what, than you were what it ſhould prove

I proteſs I am ſtill of the Opinion, that this is far from be
ing *Latitudinarian Divinity with a Witneſs*, as you term it
You are, I think, the firſt, and in likelihood will be the laſt
Man that ever denied it And herein I ſuppoſe you would not
have been ſingular, had you not been tempted to it by a Deſire
of reviling me, and by a want of ſome better Materials for
Diſpute, which perhaps will ſeem ſtrange to a Man that reads
my ſecond Letter.

You think 'tis not conſiſtent with Sincerity or Uprightneſs,
for a Perſon to be in any meaſure byaſs'd by Intereſt I never
aſſerted that Uprightneſs was conſiſtent with an obſtinate, de
liberate preferring of any ſelfiſh Intereſt to a Man's Duty to
God, or that a Man could be juſtly ſaid to be an upright Man,
who allow'd himſelf in known Sin, to promote his Intereſt.
Your Conſcience has Latitude enough, to allow you to ſtrain my
Words to ſuch a ſenſe, as no one beſide your ſelf can think they
will bear, and I ſuppoſe you thought it would be for your Intereſt to do ſo, and therefore, I fear, muſt be here ſelf-con-
demn'd

I ſuppoſed the Matter under Conſideration to be diſputable,
and that there may be ſome plauſible Reaſons alledg'd on the
wrong ſide, but that with all temporal Intereſt was apparently
for it, and I ſaid, I thought *Intereſt* might, in this Caſe, *give
a Byaſs, in ſome meaſure, to Men who were yet truly ſincere and
upright*, that is, not through their Wilfulneſs, while they reſolve to purſue their Intereſt, right or wrong, or tho they are
convinc'd that their Intereſt and Duty will not conſiſt, but
through meer Inadvertency They are willing to have their
Intereſt and Duty conjoin'd, and to be convinc'd they are ſo,
and therefore are more eaſily prevail'd on, and ſatisfy'd by ſome
plauſible Arguments to believe they are. I own they ought to
watch againſt this, and to repent of it, when they diſcover
that Intereſt has thus byſs'd them : But I doubt not at all that
it may often happen, as many other Failings of a good Man's
Life, through Inadvertency or Surprize, and may therefore ſlip
his notice, and never be repented of particularly, but only
in the general And in that Caſe, I make no doubt, where
the Tenour of a Man's Life is conſonant to the Divine Law,
that ſuch Failings and Infirmities are forgiven him And I
am

am very much inclin'd to that *Latitudinarian Divinity* (if it must be fo nam'd) that judges of Mens Integrity not by a fingle Act, which may not it felf be upright, but by the prevailing Bent of a Man's Heart, and the main Courfe of his Life. I will ask you, Whether you do not think St. *Peter* was a fincere and upright Man? and yet was fomewhat mov'd by Vogue and Intereft (that is, fome kind of finful Selfifhnefs) when he, with feveral more, acted in that manner, mention'd, *Gal.* 2. 11, 12, 13, 14. when St. *Paul* fays exprefly, they walked not uprightly? Or I might ask, Whether you do not believe that the two Sons of *Zebedee* were fincere and upright Man, and yet were byafs'd by Intereft in their Petition to our Lord, to fit the one on his Right Hand, and the other on his Left, in his Kingdom? I might ask you, Whether you do not think a finful Intereft, in fome or other of the Branches of it, is not the main Temptation that occafions the Sins and Failings of fincere and upright Men? I am inclin'd to think this is one way or other at the bottom of moft Sins And therefore fince I judge the Sincere and Upright do daily fin, I think it not unreafonable to fuppofe this in fome meafure to byafs them. Again, do you Believe, Sir, that there is no fincere and upright Man that ever fins, in not being as charitable as he ought to the Poor? Or do you think, that if fuch an one may poffibly fin in this Refpect, he is not therein, in the leaft meafure, byafs'd by Intereft? Or do you think that every fincere Man, in a way of Trade, does not in the leaft meafure exceed due bounds in feeking the World? or that if he does, he is not byafs'd by Intereft to do fo? Or will you fay, that all thofe famous Writers of your own Church were not in the leaft meafure byafs'd by Intereft, who wrote with fo much Heat and Earneftnefs for Paffive Obedience? or thofe who have fince renounc'd that Doctrine? or will you fay, that all thofe who were in the leaft meafure byafs'd by Intereft, were not fincere and upright? Do you think the Nonjurors are the only fincere and upright Men in the Nation? Or do you think that all thofe, who declar'd that it is not lawful, on any pretence whatever, to take up Arms againft the King, had not their Judgments in the leaft meafure byafs'd by Intereft, when they judg'd that Declaration to contain only a Truth? In fine, Sir, I ask you, Whether you are willing to have your Sincerity and Uprightnefs try'd by your own Rule at the great Day? Are you willing that God fhould condemn you for ever as infincere and hypocritical, if you can then be found to have ever been (fuppofe in the laft 20 or 30 Years paft of your Life) IN THE LEAST MEASURE byafs'd by Intereft, of which you have not particularly

larly repented ? Dare you fay this ? For my own part I dar
not for ten Thoufand Worlds , but defire to rely on the Merc
of God for the Forgivenefs of thofe manifold Failings I ma
have been guilty of in this kind, which I obferv d not at the
particular times, and have not therefore been able to repent o
particularly fince. Nor are my Notions peculiar in this re
fpeĉt Do not your own chief Writers allow as much ? I hav
had the Curiofity on this Occafion to confult fome eminen
Writers of your own , fuch as Arch Bifhop *Tillotfon*, Dr Shei
lock, Dr *Barrow*, and Dr *Lucas* , and fhall be ready to pre
duce their Teftimonies if you call for them . And the only Rea
fon why I do it not now, is, becaufe they would fwell my An
fwer too much ; and the Cafe is fo plain as to render it nee
lefs I fhall therefore content my felf with the Teftimony o
Dr *Hammond*, Practical Catechifm, *Lib 2 Seĉt.* 1 Where h
has thefe words, " But the Truth is, as long as we live here
" and carry this Flefh about us, fomewhat of Carnality there
" will remain to be duly pu 'd out, and fo alfo fome Dou
" blings, fome Reliques of Impourity, fomewhat of my felf
" my own Credit, *my own Intereft*, ftill *fecretly interpofing* it
" my Godliett Aĉtions. But thefe (fo they be not fuffer d to
" reign, to be the chief Mafters in me, to carry the main or
" my Aĉtions after them) may be reconcileable with a good
" Eftate , as humane Frailties, not wafting Sins. Nay, I do
not eafily believe your own Divinity will difallow of this, no
can i think fo meanly of your Underftanding, as to ouef ted
whether you did not perceive my Meaning And, Sir, if w
have ever yet d been wilfully to trangue r , think for the
Godfall; nor a Injury without particular Repent
nor a fatisfaction as publick as the Injury it felf
You … unto me from the Commo of People, who
the, worfe power of Minfineere, all dge this, that it was
in an mefur be byafs'd by Intereft, but truly I judge th
Exprefhon is Hyperbolical, unlefs they mean thus, that he w
not knowingly and wilfully be fo byafs'd And I very muc
queftion whether any fingle Virtue (and particularly a Contemp
of the World) be ever perfeĉt in any Man in this Life Am
yet your Hypothefis is built on that Opinion
You fay, *Our Saviour plainly affirms*, Mat 6 24 *he can
ferve God and Mammon*, *but you, Sir, on the contrary, teach in
effeĉt, yet in force God and Mammon* for to be byafs'd by Int
reft, fo far as to be kept from difcovering and praĉtifing ou
Duty to God, is no other than to ferve Mammon But do not
allow, that a Man is to be denominated not from fingle Aĉt
and unoblerv'd Frailties, but from the general and main bent

of

of his Life and Actions ? Has not every true Servant of God Work and Bufinefs to do in this Matter, to mortify thofe worldly Affections that ftill remain *in fome meafure in him*, tho the full Power and Dominion of them be broken ? Let Dr *Hammond* be here confulted, who knowing the Truth of what I afferted, and which I have fet down from him, thus paraphrafes that Text, *Mat* 6 24. " Even fo the tending and atchieving of Wealth, " doing nothing but may in the Eye of the World tend to the " Increafe of Riches, is not reconcileable with the ferving of " God, doing what Chrift requires of us

And he that will confult the *Synopfis Criticorum*, will find o-thers, and particularly *Gronus*, thus to expound the Text, and I perfwade my felf you are the firft Man in the World who ever interpreted that Text, fo as to exclude from being the Ser-vants of God, thofe who had any finful Regard to the World , and by the fame kind of Reafoning, you might prove from *Rom* 6 16. that no Sin is confiftent with a Man's being a Ser-vant of Righteoufnefs, and fhew your Unmercifulnefs to all Mankind And now I need not confider diftinctly the wild Suppofitions you put, which no more concern me than the Man in the Moon

But only as you are pleas'd before you leave this, and feve-ral times afterward, to reflect on me and my Party, as byafs'd by Intereft, I befeech you next time to let me know what Inte-reft the Generality of Diffent is can be fuppos'd bial'd by , who by their Diffent put themfelves, as you know, to a Charge in feveral Refpect, whilft the other wife rect from Or rt but at t, i declare plainly, but as to th m declare to a convinced that I know the convince, that I do th t does not fhall by d ado it, t ur ub unit the Conviction of my Mind I al aft e that it fhall not hinder the Impartiality of my Judgment I beg Pardon of my Reader for detaining him th s I ou m I plain a Cafe I can as eafily pafs over an impertinent Ramble as another, but when tis fet out with a grave and folemn Air, and attended with the Charge of falfe Doctrine, 'tis really provoking, and will apologize for a longer Anfwer And as to you, Sir, I fhall only pity you, and pray God throughly to convince and gracioufly pardon you

In the next place you take notice of what I fay, *That the Diffenters are not all on their part to end the Divifion* You fay, *You would fain know for what Reafon* And that you may eafily know from my Letter, wherein I have fpoken plainly enough, and therefore can't but wonder at fuch Difcourfe as this from

you

you. You fay, *There are no hard or finful Terms impos'd on us*, that is, I fuppofe, none that you think fo, but, you know, we think otherwife, on fuch Reafons as you have not, as yet, thought fit to anfwer And therefore the reſt of your Para-graph is ufelefs

You put it to me, *Whether the old Puritans, or Nonconform ſt*, *were not as truly zealous againſt Popery as we can be* Well, let it be fo, and neither of us can be charg'd with want of Zeal a-gainſt Popery You fay, *Albeit they did diflike many things as we do, yet they judg'd it then bounden Duty not to begin a Diviſion from the Church, becaufe they plainly forefw it would give Ad-vantages to Popery* And you think this Difference between them and us is owing to this, that they were fincere and up-right, and we are not. But nothing can be more unreafonal e than this Difcourfe For, (1) The very Terms of Conformity were purpofely made harder in 1662 than they were to the old Puritans. (2) Since you own they were fincere and up-right, and yet fcrupled fever d things, you muſt own that there are hard and difficult Terms impos'd on us, even fuch as up-right Men may judge fo (3) The fruitlefs Endeavours of the old Puritans to gain a Reformation while they continued in the Church, is a Vindication of us in Leaving it I think 'tis one thing that thofe of your o wn fide do generally advance, that Men who are diſſatisfy'd in a Church, fhould not raſhly make a Separation, but fhould firſt try all humble and proper Methods to prevail on Church-Rulers to mend the things that need Re-formation This was long done by our Predeceffors, but no-thing could be gain'd, but on the contrary, the Cafe is left worfe than it was before, and they now think the Conduct more juſt and reafonable (4) The Nonconform ſt of old, t o they often fuffer'd in one place, they were yet ca-pable of being ufeful in another, in the Church of England whereas all that are of their Principles are now by the B th' Uniform Act render'd utterly incapable of any Service in th' Church. And in truth the Conduct of the old Puritans and the prefent Diffenters, is not different as to the main They were willing to keep in the Church as long as they could, and we, notwithſtanding our being violently and unjuſtly thruſt out by our Brethren, are willing even to return to them, and have all along ſhown it, tho they will not fuffer us And methinks, when we are forcibly thruſt out, and the Door is fhut with a de-fign to keep us out, 'tis not like fincere Dealing to rail at us for not coming in Befides, the Advantage the Papiſt gain by our Divifions is not directly from us, nor is it amongſt us We do not in the leaſt fwerve toward Popery, nor have they been able to gain Profelytes among us , but they practis'd on the fame fort of Men for gaining Profelytes, as they h'd before for ma-king a Divifion We are not, for our Divifion, one whit the more inclin'd to their Doctrines, or backward to yield the moft hearty Affiftance againft their Caufe The Advantages then that the Papifts gain by our Divifions are fuch as thefe , That they have a plaufible Pretence to ufe with People, to recom-mend the Authority and Power which they pretend to over Mens Confciences, is they do from the Differences among Pro-teftants in general Or they can the more eafily work on our intereft Adverfaries, who from a Spirit of Oppofition are wil-ling to depart as far as they can from us, tho at the fame time they make Advances toward them Or elfe having made a Divifion among us, they have ftir'd up our Brethren to plunder and undo us, that fo the Hands of fuch as were as zealous (it can) as any againft them, might in a great meafure be difa-bled , and then they think when they have made ufe of one fort to crufh the other, they can the more eafily feize on the other themfelves And hereby too they think they can vindi-cate their own barbarous Perfecutions for Confcience fake. And is it not plain to you, the Diffenters have good Reafon to be forry for there having fuch Advantages as thefe by our Di-vifions ? Is it not plain they had all the Reafon, as well as In-tereft therefore to end the Divifion, and would have done it long ago, and fo have prevented their Sufferings, if they could ?

You reprefented the Diffenters as concern'd with the *Priefts,* ??? ??? of ??? ??? ??? ??? of Eng-land And I told you the Contrary, that all true Papifts withdrawing People from the Diffenters, I have feveral Inftances of your own Agreement with them, as ??? to the purpofe than what you can all do to contrary as I fay it by, *If we agree with them in their common Defign, of ruining the Church of England, the main Bulwark of the Reform'd Religion againft Popery.* And we fay you join'd with them, in endea-vouring utterly to ruine the Diffenters, who are fo hearty Enemies to Popery as the Church of England but I do moft humbly befeech you, notwithftanding the ??? ??? ??? of your intellectuals, fo far to condefcend to ??? ??? ??? of mine, is to help me to ??? the Notion of the Church of England, as its confeffedly the Bulwark of the Reform'd Religion I then when this comes to be clear'd, your new Glofs on your Words will appear to be only, according to your Diale, a Flam, or a Quibble Is it the Doctrine, the Ceremonies, the Liturgy, or the Threefold Order of the Church of England, that is the Bul-

wark

wark of the Reformed Religion againſt Popery? The Churc
of *England*, according to ſome Mens Dialect, is one of th
moſt amphibious Creatures in the World. When any Good
done, then the Church becomes the State, and claims the Ho
nour of having done it If any Evil is done, then truly t
Church of *England* is diſtinguiſh'd from the State, and ſo
Rulers and Governour may ſhare the Diſgrace among them
To ſpeak then properly, *England* is, under God, the Bulwar
of the Reform'd Religion, as it is the moſt potent of any
the Reform'd Countries, and does contribute ſuch great Aſ
ſtance to the Proteſtant Cauſe

Now how do the Diſſenters weaken this Bulwark? Does
any Man by becoming a Diſſenter grow leſs oppoſite and ze d a
againſt Popery, or leſ ready to join in Helping Hand with t
Nation againſt it? Has it not been publickly own'd, that a
Diſſenters readily concur'd with the Church of *England* in t
late Revolution, to defeat the Deſigns of a Popiſh King? Ar
they not as zealous and hearty as any for the Proſecution of t
preſent War againſt *France*? Are not our Governours fully ſa
tisfy'd in this Matter? And if *England* be conſider d as th
Bulwark of the Reform'd Religion, 'tis not at all weaken'd in
that reſpect by the Number of Diſſenters. Nay, ſhould
the Nation fall in with us in our Principles, this Bulwark
would not be in the leaſt the weaker, but rather the ſtronger.
The only Men that I know of, whoſe Conduct weakens this
Bulwark, are they who join'd with two Popiſh Princes in their
Counſel, and in doing all the Hardſhips they could, on
Part of the Sea, and of our Nation, who were for imprifo
and plundering May, ch if t in, did their Duty, and
ſhip'd Colours, hing with t ll of their own Minds
all that th y aimed's on t t, t p o ha; Popery
n vi to t f in th y, via, in ſime the ſame Princip
ave b en of lic ntion, un to r iv then old Prictic
Bleſſed be God who his not a in u a Prey to their Teeth

You a k if what I ſay b tru, ſ ut all Parties think themſelv
in the right, n t l e to brec her of then Mind, why we d
think fit to follow ſ n Pr n, m w n the Quakers to our ſel
ſince we differ more from th m th n n y? Now according to th
Obſervation I have been hitherto able to make, I could n
t but that the Diſſent r w wiling to draw n both ſid
I don't perceive that th y make it their buſineſs to perſuad
Church men, until they themſelves give them Opportunit
and the ſame they m ſerve to do to any other And for
own Part, I own the Diff rence vaſtly greater between u
and Quaker a Papiſt, than between us and you, ſo I ſhou
not

much rather convince one Quaker or Papift of the Goodnefs of our Caufe, than ten fober and vertuous Church-men: and that becaufe I think the Intereft of the main things in Religion are vaftly preferable to that of a Party. Perhaps you could not fo well acquit your felf, if I fhould put it to you to give me a Reafon, why if the pretence of the Evil of Schifm be the reafon of your Heat, you, and Men of your Principles, are not more zealous to convince the Non-Jurors of their Guilt in that refpect.

As to what you fay of your Poftfcript, and your farther Defign, I am very eafy, I fhewd you, it was not difficult to run the Parallel between you and the Papifts much farther. You may ufe your Liberty as you pleafe. Such Methods will not hurt us, for tho' it would grieve one to fee the Workings of fo much Spite and Malice, yet the Management thereof, is fuch as only deferves Pity and Contempt.

You fay, You are obferved in your Teftimonies, P. 43. what ill Ground Popery got during the low Eftate of the Church of England, and the Ufurpation of Fanaticifm, efpecially of my darling Favourite, Independency. But you are the moft unhappy Man in your Guelhes of any I have met with. I have no fuch darling Favourite as you imagine. What I perceive to be a Truth I embrace, whether held by Independents or Epifcoparians, and all that know me, know I have a Latitude in all thofe Matters.

Well, I have look'd into the Place in your Teftimonies, and find very little to your purpofe. You fay, they gain'd in th'... Fanaticks (the then Late) your polite Education made you ... Church I ... Work ... to be ... of in their high Watch ... were acquired not time to end that Nation. And did they not join with the Church of England there exerted oppofing the Diffenters? Aolort Ment ... de Sumone. Account may be true for ought I know, but I am not much inclin'd to believe it on his word. And what if there were Papifts that ferv'd the Parliament against the King, were there not likewife that ferv'd on the other fide? And what if Mr. Lauder fays the Papifts did penn by the ... themfelves under the Vizor of Independency. Are they not ready to do the like under any Vizor? Or have they not appear'd without any Vizor at all fince the Church of England recover'd her felf out of her fo ... State? What tho' Dr. Burly courted Oliver with grofs Flattery, were not others of the Church of England courted by the Papifts in like manner? Why elfe was a Cardinals Hat offer'd to an Arch Bifhop? Or why did the Benedictine Monk Mont...

dus fo highly flatter Arch biſhop *Laud*, as it appears he did the Arch Biſhop's Anſwer to him, publiſh'd by *Le Clerc*, the Beginning of his Edition of the Fathers which liv'd in the Apoſtle's Times? Or why did the Papiſts boaſt ſo much in t. A Bp's Time, of the Steps made towards them? Why did t. Jeſuit (Dr. *Heylin* mentions in A Bp. *Laud's* Life, p. 416 boaſt, " That the Articles of the Church of *England* ſeem t " tient, or ambitious rather of ſome Senſe, wherein they m " ſeem Catholick? Why was it pretended by their Part " That the Univerſities, Biſhops and Divines of this Realm " did daily embrace Catholick Opinions, tho they profeſs'd no " ſo much with Mouth or Pen, *for fear of the Puritanes ?* Ibid And a great deal more may Le ſeen to the ſame purpoſe in the part of the Doctor's Hiſtory. In fine, You give us a might Evidence of the vaſt Ground Popery got in that time, *viz* no leſs than *One Hundred and Fifty Perfons* are mention'd, as re concil'd to *Rome* in the Year 1652. This might be a grea thing then, but I fear it has been ſo vaſtly out-done for ſevera Years together, ſince the Church of *England* got out of its lov Eſtate, and this Bulwark was up, that it hardly deſerves to be remember'd, much leſs that ſuch Uſe as this ſhould be made of it

You ſay, there is a *Popiſh Deſign at the Bottom of the Noiſe and Clamour which has been lately made about High and Low Church-men.* And indeed I fear this Noiſe and Clamour is too truly bottom'd on ſome Popiſh Deſign, not of theirs, on whom you would charge it, but of quite another ſort of Men. Good Sir, do you not think the Papiſts have ſome Deſign working, according to the Reſtleſsneſs of their Humour? They uſe not to work alone, who are they then that join with them? Are they not the Ja cobites, and thoſe call'd High Church-men? Alas, what has been ſo publickly obſerv'd, and ſo openly ſpoken of, can't be conceal'd, and therefore I can't but with you think, there is indeed ſome Popiſh Deſign at the Bottom of the Difference, which one part of the Church of *England* has made by their violent Counfels, the Succeſs of which would have been no ſmall Joy to their good Friends of St. *Germins*, and their Abet tors I value not the Names themſelves. Call them what you pleaſe

Is there not manifeſtly a Foundation for a Diſtinction among your ſelves? If not, whence are the mighty Struggles at Ele ction? His not the Diſtinction been coin'd among your ſelves? And have you not wrote againſt one another under thoſe Names? And therefore if there be really no Foundation for Diſtinction among you, you are much to be admir'd, I confeſs, that you

are

are ſo earneſtly contending about a little *Goats Wool.* Whether your Account of your ſelf, and your apparent Conduct do agree, I leave to the Reader to judge from your
Writings. I never took you for a Pluraliſt, as you tax me,
nor is there any thing in my words that gives any Intima-
tion of it.

I had ſaid (*L* 2. *p.* 48) *'Tis plain who are now moſt ſerviceable
to the Popiſh Cauſe, even thoſe who are united in Counſels with
them, as the Jacobites and High Church-men actually are, and
that in oppoſition to the Diſſenters and Moderate Church-men.
And there is evidently more Danger from the Oppoſition of the High
Church, againſt the Moderate Church-men, than from any Diſagree-
ment between them and the Diſſenters And 'tis the Union of theſe
two that has kept out Popery, which had otherwiſe overflown the
Nation*

With Reference to this Diſtinction, you ſay, *it was brought
up by the Enemies of your Church.* Suppoſing it were, you are
ſerv'd then only in your own kind, who ſo freely uſe the moſt
abuſive Expreſſions of the Diſſenters. But there is no manner
of Ground for you to alledge this You ſay indeed, *there is
no ſolid Reaſon for the Diſtinction, but it carries in it ſelf down-
right Nonſenſe* But if there be a Difference between you, and
the Church of *England* is really divided into two different Parties, contending and quarrelling with one another, and pur-
ſuing oppoſite Intereſts every where, this muſt be a *ſolid Reaſon for a Diſtinction* ; and he muſt be blind indeed that can't
ſee this to be the Caſe at this Day Now, how would you have
a Man diſtinguiſh theſe two Parties? I call'd them by ſuch
Names as they are generally call'd by, and as many on both
ſides own, and I think that was the way to be underſtood.
But where is the downright Nonſenſe ? Are you all agreed a-
bout the Things in Controverſy? Are not ſome much higher
in their Notions about the Things controverted, looking on
them as eſſential, and fundamental , and others thinking them
only tolerable, and wiſhing them laid aſide ? Has there not
been all along two ſuch Parties in the Church ? Again, are not
ſome high in their Notions about Perſecution, and the forcible
Methods of preſſing thoſe things on the Diſſenters; while o-
thers are for our full Liberty? Are not ſome high-flown in
paſſing damning Sentences on us, while others charitably love
us as Chriſtians and Brethren ? Again, Do not many plead a-
gainſt any Alterations, as tho there were no good and juſt Occaſion for them , while others plead for Alteration, and ſay
there is a good and juſt Occaſion? You may ſhuffle, if you
will, and diſſemble this, but all Men know it to be true, that
it

it is thus among all Sorts and Ranks of you. Do not you your
felf diftinguifh Bifhops in, and Bifhops of the Church ? Do
you not cut off a great many Church-men, by denying them to
be true Church-men, or true Members of the Church of *En*
gland ? You really in effect grant the Diftinction, but only according to the Mode of High-Church, and a pretty Jingle,
Low-Church is No-Church   This, Sir, I hope, will help you
to underftand my Meaning, which was fufficiently plain   It
concerns not me to determine which Side acts moft fairly,
what I obferv'd is a known Truth, That thefe High Church-
men do actually join with the Jacobites and Papifts   And as
they were fuch kind of Men that loaded us at firft with Hard-
fhips, and made the Divifion, and have kept it up, fo it has
been the Party which oppos'd them , v z The Moderate
or Low Church-men, who have prevented the Effect and Ac-
complifhment of their Defigns

You next confider what things are fundamental and neceffary,
and fo not to be alter d on any Occafion, p 16   And here the
firft thing is the *Threefold Order of Miniftry*   But here the
Queftion is, Whether you may not keep your Fundamental,
and yet indulge others a Liberty of not looking on it as a
Fundamental ? (Whether if this be a Truth, it is fuch an one
that it is abfolutely neceffary every Minifte fhould believe it)
You fay, *No one can be efteem'd a true Member of the Church of*
England, *that is not fincerely ready to part with his Life, rather*
than the faid Apoftolical Confitution   But why then do you
urge the Diffenters, who would not part with their Live
you may be fure, at fuch a rate, to become Members of the
Church of *E*   If they followed the Example you mention'd of the old Puritans, and conform'd, they could not
be had on to the Mafs   of the Church of *England*,
therefore, in my mind they had better be in fuch a Church
of which they may be look'd on to be true Members

Next you add, *As for Liturgies, and Forms of Prayer, tho' they*
are not abfolutely neceffary in themfelves, (which I am glad to
hear of, for Rifhn fs in Prayer may then be prevented without
them) yet, " It becomes neceffary (to ufe Mr *Calvin*'s words)
" that the publick Prayers fhould be ftated or fix'd, from which
" it may not be lawful for any Minifter to vary, in the Lxer-
" cife of his Function, as well in confideration of the Weak-
" nefs and Ignorance of fome, as that it may appear how all
" Churches agree among themfelves, and withall that
" there may be a ftop put to the giddy Inconftancies of fome who
" affect Novelties   And becaufe you think thefe three Reafons
will be always of force, it will be neceffary always to retain
                                                                your

our excellent Liturgy, tho you fhould charitably condefcend to the Alteration of fome Expreſſions in it In your Teſtimonies, *p.* 4 you cite part of this Teſtimony, and there you make *Calvin* not to fay, IT IS NECESSARY, is you do here, but only that HE HIGHLY APPROV'D, which is moſt agreeable to his words, *valde probo* but if you l'ow of Mr Calvin's Argument, you muſt wholly exclude conceiv'd Prayer, which I think you ought not to do, becauſe of what I have alledg'd to fhew the Neceſſity thereof, where Forms are uſ'd And befides you condemn your own Church, which allows Miniſters to uſe conceiv'd Prayer before their Sermons, as I obſerv'd, 15 of my 1ſt Letter. But let us conſider the particular Reaſons themſelves His firſt Reaſon is, *the Confideration of the Weakneſs and Ignorance of fome* And 'tis very poſſible that others, if they had liv'd in his Time, would have thought this Confideration of great moment in the behalf of Forms When the Alteration was mad in our Churches, it can't be wonder'd at, that there were many weak and ignorant Perfons, who kept in their Livings, and if they had not, all their Vacancies could not preſently have been fill'd up with better : So that if there had not been fome fuch Proviſion as this, there muſt have been no Prayers at all in fome Pariſhes, and Mr. *Calvin* complains of the Scarcity of able Miniſters at that time in that very Lpiſtle. And if that was a Reaſon then, fure you will not ſay that this is the Cafe of the Church of *England* now, that fhe is not able to ſupply all her Pariſhes with fuch as are not weak and ignorant, and therefore as this a only a Reaſon why weak Perfons, there a uſ' Form, he is to be ſippd'd Cur as he taken to keep this out

His ſecond Reaſon a, *If ... may provi ..., when ... a ... the Camſles agree among themſelves* For my Part, tro I highly value Mr Calvin Memory, yet I can't ſay, that I think this Argument concluſive For I think it may certainly appear, that Churches do agree as far as is neceſſary without fuch Forms And why in account of the ordinary Matter of the feveral Churches Prayers, tho there be no Forms uſ'd, is not fufficient to anſwer that end, I do not as yet underſtand

Mr *Calvin's* laſt Reaſon is, *That there may be a ſtop put to the giddy Lightneſs of fome who affect Noveltes* But 'tis very ſtrange if Care may not be taken to prevent this without Forms - For my part, I proteſt, I'm as much an Enemy to the mixing any novel Fancies with Publick Devotions, is the moſt zealous Advocates for Forms can be, and if Men are not capable of difcharging that Duty (or willing to do it) without affecting fuch Novelties, I think they are very unfit to be admitted to the facred Office. B Yo'

You ſay, *No true Church-man can come ſo low as to part with y*
Liturgy But I believe I do not miſtake the Minds of lor
Church-men, who uſe it as impos'd, and judging it tolerab
and who would not, if left to themſelves, preſer the uſe of y
But what kind of Church-men do you urge us to be, when y
perſwade us to come into the Church, notwithſtanding or
Diſlike of ſome things ? True Church-men you would not a
low us to be, ſuppoſing we come not up to your Eſteem of th
Liturgy, and therefore I think you had better be eaſy, to let u
continue true Diſſenters

You ſay, That *all other Rites and Ceremonies us'd in you*
Church, and ſcruſled at by the Diſſenters (as the Croſs in Baptiſm
God-fathers, and God-Mothers, Kneeling at the Sacrament, Sur
ply ce, &c) are ſo far not fundamental or neceſſary, as to admit of
Alteration on weighty and juſt Occaſions And therefore you can
not but think that every true Church-man is charitably diſpos'd
to condeſcend to ſuch Alterations as ſhall be requiſite on weighty an
juſt Occaſions.

I ſhould be heartily glad to ſee ſome Evidence of this Charity in all true Church-men. But 'tis ſufficiently plain, this
Conceſſion ſignifies juſt nothing . For as you have hitherto, ſo
for ought I can find (and eſpecially if I may judge by your
ſelf) you are reſolv'd to deny that any ſuch weighty and juſt
Occaſion has, or will ever come . So that this is very little to
the Satisfaction of the Diſſenters.

You next proceed to enquire, *What is or is not a juſt Occaſion*
for ſuch Alterations? Give me leave (before I proceed to conſi
der what you ſay particularly on this Head) to take notice to
you what I look on as a juſt Occaſion for making Alterations
(1) If there be any things confeſſedly amiſs in any Church,
there is juſt occaſion for Alterations, by mending thoſe things
which are amiſs And that there are ſome things amiſs in
your Church, I think will not be denied Your Lay-Chancel-
lors, want of Diſcipline with reference to ſcandalous Perſons,
(whether Clergy or Laity) do certainly call for Reformation
Why do you not therefore ſet about making Alterations in
theſe ? For my part, I really judge you can't in any Method
better ſerve your own Cauſe, and I profeſs, tho you ſhould
hereby leſſen the Number of Diſſenters, and ſhould not widen
your Door ſo far as to ſatisfie me to come in, I ſhould yet hear
tily rejoice, from the great Love I have to Reformation.
(2) Suppoſe the things impos'd as indifferent, are by a great
Number of Chriſtians judg'd ſinful, and from the Impoſition
does ariſe (as there then neceſſarily muſt) Diſcord and Strife ,
there is then Reaſon for altering the Impoſition For tho the

things

things fhould really prove lawful, yet the Impofers can't them felves be free from Blame, inafmuch as they do by this means lay a Snare for them, and without any neceffity give occafion for that Strife And this is the Cafe as to many things enjoin'd , we judge them unlawful, you fay they are indifferent , and therefore without neceffity you breed Difcords and Strife among Chriftians. So that, tho 'twere fuppos'd the Impofers had really a Title to a much larger Power than my Notions do allow, yet I can't fee how they can excufe themfelves from blame while they infift on fuch things Let me now confider what *you* fay concerning a juft Occafion of Alterations You fay, *Nothing elfe can be fuch, but the attaining a greater Good by them than can be attain'd without them.* * Now here you think *'tis to be confider'd, whether the Alterations contended for by us, will not do as much hurt one way, by fhutting the Door clofer than needs be againft the Papifts, as it may do good, by opening the Door wider than needs be to the Diffenters.* But the Anfwer to this is eafy, Set the Door as Chrift and his Apoftles left it, and then the blame will lie on thofe who do not come in on either fide. But 'tis a little ftrange that you, Sir, who can't but underftand the monftrous Opinions of the Papifts, fhould think that thefe little things in difpute fhould, if laid afide, be any Hinderance to the Papifts coming over to us, fuppofing them convinc'd of the great Matters afferted by Proteftants in oppofition to them. Will a Man that believes the Doctrines of Tranfubftantiation, Infallibility, Purgatory, *&c.* to be falfe and abominable, remain in that Church for the fake of a Surplice, the Sign of the Crofs, *&c.* I profefs you amaze me by fuch Difcourfe : If you will not fee you are to be pitied, I will not fay for your Intellectuals, but for your Obftinacy. But the thing is plain, that the Difference between you and the Papifts is in fuch vaftly greater things, that the keeping of thefe little Matters, is the moft inconfiderable Trifle in the World toward the gaining of them, but I think our Differences are fo fmall, as that they may eafily be accomodated. So that here is a greater Good that is really very probable, and the Danger on the other hand is grounded only on a trifling Surmize.

But you go on, and tell us, that *to this muft be added, that fuch Alterations may become a ftumbling Block to fome that are at prefent of our own Communion, and who may poffibly be fo weak as to think more highly of the things to be laid afide than they ought , and therefore go over from us to the Papifts on that account.*

I'm glad you fpeak this, I doubt not it would have been reckon'd a Crime in any one elfe, to fay, That *fome of your Communion are fo weak, as to think more highly of thofe things*

that

than they ought And hence I fee that the Church-men, accor
ding to you felf, are not all agreed, any more than the Dif
fenters, and that it were eafy to make fuch a Reprefentatio
of you, as you have done of us, and that on better Ground
than you can pretend ; as you may fee by comparing what
fay in my Third Letter But I would fain know what you
mean, *by their thinking of thefe things more highly than the
ought* I can't fee but that if they think of them fo highly
as to be willing to fwallow all the monftrous Doctrines, fu
perftitions, and Idolatries of the Romifh Church with them
(which is the Cafe you put) they muft look upon them a
fundamental and effential things with a Witnefs, and no
as indifferent and alterable, and confequently they muf
preflife thefe Commandments of Men as taught for Doctrines
And you fay your felf, *p. 15.* of your Firft Letter to a Diffen
ting Parifhioner, *That Chrift rebukes the Jews for teaching fuch
their Traditions* (as are mentioned, *Mat.* 15.) *for Doctrines,
that is, making them of equal Obligation and Neceffity with the
commandments of God* Hence therefore I infer, that fuch
an Affertion of thefe Things is finful, and confequently your own Argument does condemn you, and fhews the
Neceffity of thofe Alterations againft which you alledge it.
For hence tis plain, that the retaining thefe Things does
really tend to lead fuch Men into Sin, while they ufe them
in fuch a manner, and by this means the Confciences of
your weak Brethren among your felves are wounded. I
have often thought this Argument had weight in it, but
did not expect you would ever give me fuch Occafion to
make Ufe of it. You may try how you can get off it.

But I will be fo free with you as to ask you one Queftion,
and that is, Whether you do in your Confcience believe that
any one good Chriftian in your Communion would by fuch Alterations be tempted to believe Tranfubftantiation, &c. and fo
to go over from you to the Church of *Rome*? In my Appre-
henfion all thofe Perfons you can fuppofe your felves in danger of loofing, are fuch, as are real Blemifhes in any Church,
and fhould be rather tu'nd out than kept in. And do you think
that by Alterations you fhall gain none from the Diffenters
worth having? Why then are you fo defirous to perfwade
them to come over to you?

1ft You fay the furtheft Alterations *that can with
a good Confcience be confented to by a true Church-man, even
in times not needing, is only this, that every Perfon may
be left* ... *in his own Perfwafion in thefe
... particulars, or have none, to have his
Ch'd*

Child fign'd or not fign'd with the Crofs Here I think I may
affure you that I know feveral who differ fo much from you,
as to give a juft Foundation for their being call'd Low-Church-
men But let that pals. I fay then, if this be the loweft, and
you have fully expreff'd your mind, it will not do, for the ut-
moft you go, is to leave Parents it liberty but for ought I
fee, the Minifter muft be oblig'd to comply with the Parents defire, let it be one way or the other. If you intend more than
you expiels, *viz* that the Minifter fhall have his Liberty
alfo, and where Minifter and Parent can t agree, it fhall be allow-
ed the Parent to apply himfelf to another who will agree to his
Defire ; this will fully remove this Part of our Difference.

2dly. You fay *there can be no good or juft Occafion, but when a*
CERTAIN *Good will follow.* I thought fuch fhort-fighted
Creatures, as we all are, muft often act on far lefs Affurance
than what you demand. A probable Good may be reafon en ugh
for Alterations. But any one may fee what all this means,
and you fufficiently difcover elfewhere your averfion to any Alterations whatever. But fuppofe there were no other certain
Good did enfue but the reforming your felves, and the rendring
the Diffenters inexcufable, this were a juft and weighty Occafion enough for Alterations, as the Cafe ftands with you.

But you fay *it muft be confider'd,* (1) *Whether it will not be-*
come requifite to this End, that all the Diffenters that are come to
Years of Difcretion fhould in the firft Place give it under their
Han s, that fuch Alterations and Conceffions will fatisfy them,
and fhould by fome or other valuable Obligation ftrictly engage
themfelves to leave off their Separation, as foon as ever the faid
Conceffions fhould be made, &c. Well then, if this is a Matter
to be confider'd, and all were of your Mind, I would for ever
abandon all thoughts of Union Muft this be the only thing
to be reckon'd a certain Good ? Suppofe one half of the Diffenters were gain d, were it not worth your while to make Alterations, to refcue fo many Souls out of that State of Damnation, which you apprehend them in on the account of their
Schifm ? If you think not, you are of a Mind as opp fite to
his, whofe Minifters you pretend to be, as is Darknefs to Light.
Intereft will oblige the Diffenters to fall in with thofe Conceffions they feek for, and therefore there is no need of
our giving it under our Hands. What valuable Obligation you
mean I know not, but imagine it muft be fuch as you would
not care Church-Men fhould come under, not to return again to
their old Encroachments.

(2) You fay 'tis to be confider d, whether though all the pre
fent Diffenters that are at Age fhould hereby be brought over, yet

- it

it may not be reasonably fear'd, that in 10 or 12 Years a new G-
neration may arise (in short) *of Dissenters* Suppose it, yet you
have sav'd the Present according to your own Notions But I
think 'tis not to be doubted, that if Church-Communion b
set on a Scripture-Foot, there will be no Danger of this among
serious Christians Human Impositions tend to Division, Di
vine only to Peace and Unity But you will shew that *this is a*
supposable Case from what has been already, and here you tell
me a Story which you have heard But perhaps you kno
not when, nor where you heard it The Story I alledg d I h d,
as I said, from a Person of Credit, and could easily have
most solemnly confirm d, if needful, and contains nothing
credible in it, and perhaps your self are not unacquainted
with an English Bishop much of the same mind I have hear
as much of him, but not having that Evidence I had in th
other Case, did not mention him But you tell us a Story n r
very credible, and do not so much as tell us, whether you be
lieve it your self. 'Tis not easy to believe Men would n t
keep a Copy by them of what they deliver'd, nor is it proba
ble they would begin with specifying the Alterations they de
sir'd But such sort of Stories the Dissenters are us'd to, and
much such another you may see confuted in the Appendix to
Mr Baxter's Life, *p* 108 But then you argue in the next
from what I say, that 'tis one receiv'd Principle of the
Di enters, that no Man or Body of Men are the Standard of
Truth, and that their Notions are not to be enslav'd to the
Sentiments of others And I hum'
ask you, Whether this is not a receiv'd Principle of all Pr
testant of the Church of L d, and even, Sir, of y
self Whom the Man, or which is the Body of Men y
esteem the Standard of Truth? Whom do you so value a to
enslave your Notions to their Sentiments You talk like a Man
hugely fond of Infallibility, Please to inform the World
when you know, where to fix it In the mean while give me
leave to remember the Direction of Christ, who is indeed the
Standard of Truth, *call no Man Father on Earth*, Matt 23 9
As to what you add, I think I never did desire an Alteration of
any Fundamental in Religion, unless you are to be Judge
    You say, *That I may here learn how far 'tis in the Power*
of the Church to do this in Discussion But I see no Power the Church
has to alter one thing establish'd by Act of Parliament I thin k
God for it, or the poor Dissenters must have been in as
sorry a Case as ever The Church may do much to procure
Alterations, but I never could hear of any Instance of a gene
ral Willingness and Readiness to do any thing, except wha
                                                          th r

they were afraid of being over-run with Popery in King *James* II's Time. And so you may easily judge what I mean by saying, *'Tis in the Power of the Parliament to remove those things which keep the Breach wide open* That is, that is the Obligation that lies on those of the establish'd Communion, to observe the things in dispute, is from the Parliament, t ev can alter the Obligation at Pleasure And since you shew such an Aversion to Alterations, I can t think it would be a Reflection on the Wisdom of the Parliament, to take that Matter into Consideration , and to endeavour by New Acts to unite those whom former Acts have separated one from another

You are free to apply those Words, *APOSTOLICAL CONSTITUTION*, to what you please I assure you I neither believe the three-fold Order to be such, nor will I ever so subscribe it , and that is now under debate between us As to the Common Prayer, I should be glad, if you reckon that also among the Apostolical Constitutions (as you seem to do) that you would direct me to the Chapter and Verse where I may find it , for I know not where to look for it at present And whatever were the Calamities that ensued on those Former Troubles in State as well as Church, they were owing to other Causes, which 'twere easy to declare, would they not be disagreeable to your self What you did in the next Paragraph is answered already

And for your Prayer, Sir, if it proceed from brotherly Love, and Christian Care I th nk so for it and 'n He tme Ply dne t Pra , d amm , the Tme t I I n pt   Pr i d G e n   t t t k th i h I P m k t m b f n s t   r c v   I n th t f a knd f P hes h ve b n t o   I mp t on me to f of you Mind , But I bless God my Integrity I hold t l, and trust that by his Grace I always shall do so, and not deliberately forsake the way of my Duty But if your Prayer is, (as I suppose any one will esteem it) designed for a Slander, as though covetous Desires were the Reason of my Non-Conformity , Don't think that your Malice will be sanctify'd by your putting it into a Prayer No, Sir, it is more heinous in the Sight of God, than if it were simply express d, while you prophane God's Name, and abuse the Duty of Prayer, to cover your Violation of his Commandment.

I think there is nothing in your Letter at the end to a Dissenting Parishioner, that needs any Answer I shall therefore only take notice of one Passage or two, that by them the Reader may judge of the rest You would represent the Dissenting Mini

sters as spreading false Reports, and not scrupling to pervert the
Councils and Designs of a Parliament, in order to enouring
their Followers in their Schism and Separation Because some
of your Parishioners have taken upon them *to tell you of some
what agitated the last Session, in opposition to your Judgment of our
Separation being a Schism or a damnable Sin* But is it not hard,
that the Dissenting Ministers must be charg'd after this Rate,
for a little Mistake in the words of those, *Whose Business (*
you tell us) *lies most among the bellowing of Cattle and Fleecing
of Sheep ?* Put but the word Parliament instead of Session, and
all is easy and clear, and you know it to be most true And
could you not easily have help'd them over this Difficul
ty ? I think you might *without much spending your self, or being
spent for them* And I suppose there may be the like Reason
for your talking, of t he Reports, industriously spread abroad,
concerning wat part between your most worthy Diocesan and
your self at his late Visitation. Some improper Term, it is
likely, has been used by an honest Country-man, who pretends
not to nicety of Language, and that you think a sufficient
ground for you to make complaint of false Reports. I am not
concern'd to know what pass'd between you and your Diocesan,
for whom I have a great value, and who, I persuade my self,
is a Man of too moderate Councils and Spirit to approve of
your hostile and turbulent Churchmen's ends, and I assure
you I rejoiced at his Preferment, and do reckon him an excell
Ornament of your Church But upon his
yet upon his good Behaviour with you, whether it may
more truly said of him, that he a eth a man, that is
Churchmen of England

And thus I think I have highly honoured this trifling S
I'd have a particular Answer. I earn stly request as you, th
would hereafter, if not for my sake, yet out of a Regard to
your own Credit and Cause, w it with more Care and By
done. If the Advice of my Friends had reach'd me before
this was near finish d, 'tis probable I had saved my self the
Labour, and not answer d but I will take leave to say, as bey
neither needed nor deserv d an Answer from,

Reverend Sir,

Your most Affectionate, and,
Faithful Servant in Christ,

James Peirce.

A Sixth Letter Addrefs'd to Dr. Wells, in Anfwer to his Letter concerning his own, and the Author's Thefes about Presbyterian Ordination.

Honoured Doctor;

HAving comply'd with your Motion of dividing the fecond Part of your Letter to Mr. D. into three diſtinct Parts, and publifh'd a Sheet in Anſwer to what you were pleas'd to advance in defence of the firſt Part, I was expecting an Anſwer from you to that Sheet at leaſt. But inſtead of that, I received yours of the 20th of January, relating only to a very ſmall and inconſiderable part of either your own, or my Letter concerning the Subject of our preſent Controverſy. You propoſe, p. 4. to conſider two or three of your own Thefes, but ſpeak to but one of them, which needed not to be ſpoken to at all. And of my 24 Theſes you conſider but two : It appears therefore to me that you reſolve to make a long Squabble, to which I aſſure you I have no Inclination. If you always take this Method, and when I truly anſwer it once, whatever you advance, you will ſplit every one of my Anſwers, after this your new Faſhion, into ſo many Parts, for ought I ſee, the longer we write, the further we are from the End of the Controverſy. I can leave it with any impartial and judicious Reader to judge, whether my Theſes are not ſufficiently clear in expreſſing what was of ſuch Moment in the Controverſy, as to deſerve a particular Anſwer, and whether the pretended reaſon of the Delay of an Anſwer to 22 of them, has any good ground, and withal whether there is any thing in your whole Letter to anſwer the Title Page, ſince you neither attempt *to prove that any one of your Propoſitions does, or any one of mine does not hold Good.*

My Fourth Letter began with theſe words *Tho I do not well underſtand the Reaſon why you are pleas'd to break your Anſwer to me (who have already ſo fully expreſs'd my mind in my Remarks) into ſo many diſtinct Parts, as you now propoſe, yet, &c.*

C   And

And with reference to this you tell me, *it seems very Strange to you that I should use such an Expreſſion, since you had taken care to make the Reaſon of your ſo doing as clear as poſſible even to my common Underſtanding*

But if you had taken due Notice of that Parentheſis, which you left out, but I have now again inſerted, it needed not to be *ſeem'd at all ſtrange to you* For when I had *ſo fully expreſs'd my Mind in my Remarks*, there could be no need to proceed ſo gradually as you propoſe. If I had ſpoken darkly and obſcurely, there might have been ſome Pretence for this; but as the Caſe ſtands, and I had giv'n a diſtinct anſwer to your Arguments, I can't ſee why you ſhould not have made it your Buſineſs to have clear'd and vindicated them all at once. I did therefore then think the Reaſon you pretended was (as you expreſs your ſelf elſewhere) *a Flam* And that in Imitation of the Learned *Chaldeans, Dan* 2. you were endeavouring by a ſhuffling anſwer to *Gain the time*, and ſtave off the main Controverſy, and ſo perhaps tire out your Adverſary, as well as your Reader And in this Apprehenſion, your laſt Letter has very much confirm'd me, as I doubt not it will many others

And thus I'm got half way through your Letter, and am now to conſider what you ſay concerning your firſt Theſis, which is,

Theſis I *The Validity of any Ordination do's immediately depend on the valid Authority of him or them, by whom is perform'd the ſaid Ordination*

In reference hereunto I had theſe Words. *Your firſt Propoſition, I conceive, do's not affect the Controverſy, for the Controverſy being, Whether Presbyters have valid Authority to ordain as well as Biſhops, if it appear they have, Presbyterian Ordination will be ſafe and valid, tho the Propoſition be granted and therefore to avoid the lengthning the Diſpute, I will anſwer your other Propoſitions on ſuppoſition of the Truth of this*

There are three things in this Paragraph, which diſpleaſe you, which I ſhall now conſider.

The firſt I ſhall conſider is, what I alledge to be the Controverſy, viz *Whether Presbyters have valid Authority to ordain as well as Biſhops* And this you deny to be the Controverſy, *foraſmuch* as both the Word [*Presbyters*] and also the Word [*Bishops*] are each capable of, and have been us'd in various Significations. But you say it is this, *Whether Presbyters, so called at the time of the Reformation, have us'd Authority in Ordaining, as well as Bishops so call'd at the said time of the Reformation?* And much to the same purpose is your 18*th* Page. But have I not fully clear'd this Matter, and taken Care to prevent this empty jingling? Have I not expresly deny'd the ambiguous Use of the word Presbyter, when taken for an Office? Lett 1 *p* 44 Have I not expresly deny'd Bishops, and Presbyters to be two distinct sacred Offices? Why do you not prove that Ambiguity which you talk so much of? and shew some good Foundation for your Distinction (*p.* 18.) *of Presbyters properly so call'd,* and the other sort of Presbyters, what ever Name you will call them by? Again, had I not expresly deny'd,

Prop. X. *That the Scripture do's distinguish two Offices, the one with the Power of Ordination, Preaching and Administring Sacraments, and the other with the Power only of Preaching, and Administring Sacraments?* Could any thing be more full than these, and several things more are to shew how I understood the Word Presbyters? Could any Man doubt of my Meaning? Is it not evident that, I endeavour to prove that there is but one sort of Presbyters mention'd in the New Testament? and that to them belongs the Power of Ordination? and consequently this Power is lodg'd in all those that are rightly ordain'd to that Sacred Office? It matters not at all what Notions they had at the Reformation. The Question is, Whether those that are ordain'd Presbyters are ordain'd to a Sacred Office instituted in the New Testament, if they are, they must have all those Powers God has annex'd to that Office, and consequently that of Ordination.

Another thing you dislike in that Paragraph, is, that I say, *Your Thesis does not affect the Controversy.* And you endeavour to prove it does, *because the Truth or Falsity of it affects the Controversy.* The Falsity thus; If the Proposition is false, then the contrary is true, and so the Controversy is needless. The Truth thus, That if the Falsity of it shews the Controversie needless, the Truth of it shews it needful. This is in short your Argument: And to it I answer, That our Controversie is not, whether the Controversie it self be needful; but whether Presbyterian Ordination be valid? And this can be only affected by a Proposition which serves to determine it, is this does not. The Falsity of it affects it only on my side,

and

and fo, if I thought fit, I might make ufe of the contrary Propofition   But it does not at all affect the Controverfie on your
fide , for if it Le falfe, no Conclufion can be juftly drawn
from it as tho it were true   And then on the other hand, the
Truth of it does not affect the Controverfie, fince, if it be
true, you can't make any ufe of it in the prefent Controverfie,
becaufe as that lies between us, it will ferve on either fide, to
fhew that Ordination valid which is perform d by Perfons t fe
appear to have valid Authority to ordain   And therefore the
this Propofition may affect other Controverfies about Ordinat
on, yet ours it does not.   And I think all Men will grant, the
that Propofition may be juftly faid not to affect a Controver
fie , which, when granted, will contribute nothing to the de
termining of the Controverfie it felf   Your own words, p 14
confirm this   ' In a word, my firft Propofition is the only
' Bafis, or Ground-truth, whereon the Validity of any Ordi
' nation, Epifcopal or Prefbyterian, is firmly to be built
Now if this be true, the Controverfie between us can never be
determin d by this Propofition , it ferves indifferently on ei
ther fide, till by other Arguments it be made appear who
have, and who have not valid Authority to ordain

Another thing you are difpleas'd with, is, *That tho I do at
prefent grant your Propofition, and fuppofe the Truth of it, yet
this is out of my meer Grace and Favour, in order to avoid
lengthening the Difpute, and not out of any neceffity I lie under
to do fo, by reafon of the Certainty and Evidence of the Truth
therein contain d*   And here you infift on my fpeaking particularly and fully to the Truth or Falfhood of that Propofition
The Reafon may here evidently fee how very diffident your
Aim is from mine   I am for fhortening the Difpute, and paf-
fing over fuch Propofitions as do not relate to it   And on the
contrary, you infift on the debating a Queftion, wholly foreign
to it.

I think, according to all the Rules of Difputation, a Refpon-
dent (and my only Bufinefs is to act that Part while I am anfwe
ing your Thefes) is bound only to grant or deny what is advanc d
by his Adverfary   And no fuch Terms were ever put on any Re
fpondent, as you pretend to put upon me   I have granted you your
Thefis, and when you find me retract my Conceffion, then you
may complain, and in the mean while make the beft ufe you can
of it, my Caufe do's not need the denial of it, and I refolve not
to give you Scope to gratify your Humour of running away from
the Point in hand   And if my granting your Propofition in this
way will not fatisfy you, you muft in fhort expect no Satisf
 action

&ction from me   I could eafily tell you how many needlefs Controverfies I hereby prevent, which would delay our coming to the Merits of the Caule . And fince I grant it you, you will beſt ſhew that it affects the Controverfie, by uſing it as a Medium to prove the Invalidity of Preſbyterian Ordination; which I do not expect to fee done by you to any good Purpoſe

Next I proceed to confider what you fay to my two firſt Thefes   The firſt is,

Th I   That no Office can be juſtly look'd on as facred which God has not appointed

This you deny, if I mean *which God himſelf has not appointed* ; but grant, if I mean *he has not appointed it himſelf, or by ſome other, divinely commiſſion d and authoriz'd*   Now my Meaning is, that no Office can be juſtly look'd upon as ſacred, which God has not appointed himſelf, or by ſome other divinely commiſſion d or authoriz'd THEREUNTO   That is, I think it very poſſible, that thoſe who may be commiſſion'd Officers and Rulers in his Church, may pretend to ſet up a new ſort of Officers therein, without any particular Inſtructions for their ſo doing, and in this Cafe, fince neither their general Commiſſion, nor any ſpecial Inſpiration, do warrant their Proceedings, I deny that any ſuch Office deviſ d by them, can be juſtly look'd on as my way propoſed , God, or therefore *as ſacred*   And conſiſtent , according to Prop. III I deny that any Office can be look'd on as ſacred, which we find not in the New Teſtament

My Second Theſis ,
II   The Offices which God has appointed, and the Powers which he has refpectively annexed to them, are infepara ble.
And as to this I need only let you know that I underſtand it in that Senfe only in which you grant it.   I own the ſame Power may be annexed to more Offices than one , but I aſſert, that no ſacred Office can be depriv d of any Power which God has annex'd to it   And this you might eafily fee by the Uſe I make of it in my fourth Propoſition, and the way in which I here apply it
And thus I have confider'd your Letter , & that item inſerted in your Poſtſcript

And

And here in the beginning you put on the Air of a wonderful mild and peaceable Perfon, willing *to undergo any Perfonal Reflections unjuftly caft upon you*. But this Air does not at all become you, who have been fo free in calling perfonal Reflections upon me, without any Shadow of Reafon, as I have fhewn in my Third Letter For my own part, I hate Perfonal Matters brought into a Controverfy, and was heartily forry I was forc'd to fay fo much on that Head in my own neceffary Defence.

That the Reader may underftand the Matter of this Poftfcript, I muft accquaint him, that whereas you did in your Letter to Mr *D* charge falfe Doctrine in Eleven Inftances on the Diflenting Teachers, I told you, you had miftaken the Diflenter In anfwer to t is, you tell us in your Examination, 7 14 *In fhort, the reafon why you fingled out thofe Eleven Particulars of falfe Doctrine rather than others, was this, Becaufe they were fuch as had been moft frequently OBJECTED to you by the Dictators with whom you had difcourfed* And to this the Second Part of my Poftfcript related, where I fay, *I have hinted in my Letter fome Reafons why I did not think the Doctor had fairly reprefented the Objections of the Diflenters he had to do with* And I am fince informed, that an Enquiry has been made among his Parifhioners, and that they difown thofe Objections, and fay they are of the Doctor's own devifing, and complain of their being abus'd by him

Your firft Anfwer to this will not feem plaufible, to thofe who confider what I have alledg'd, to fhew how improbable it is that ever any Diflenters fhould make fome of thofe Objections, and particularly thofe contain'd in your firft and laft Inftances, are fuch as I fhrewdly fufpect you can never faften upon any of them

Do you think your own Diflenting Parifhioners did not know that Mr D. receiv'd Pay ? Or could they know it, and yet make the Objection you anfwer in your laft Inftance ? And however, was it not difingenuous in you to charge fuch falfe Doctrine, when it appears plainly by feveral Paffages in your Writings, that you knew Mr D did receive Pay? But however, if you are at all fatisfy'd in their difowning thofe Objections, I fee no reafon why I fhould not be fatisfied alfo.

In your Second Anfwer, you expect your bare Word fhould be (at laft) as foon taken as is the his I leave that with you to the impartial Reader, but only I will give you this hint, that a Man who expects his Word fhould be taken by others, fhould

fident in charging others, as you have done over and over
Mr *D* and my felf, *with Untruths, down-right Quibbles,*
Flams, &c In fhort, the Liberty you take of mifreprefenting
me, gave me a Je loufy you had not truely reprefented them.

And I can eafily think you have fome other Reafon befide
what you fet down, why you, who fo freely charge Mr *D* and
my felf with Untruths, are yet fo fparing of the Names of o-
thers

But I fee you have left room ftill for another Evafion, for
you fay, *You are able to name the Perfons, who either in their*
Difcourfes have exprefly made ufe of the faid Objections, or elfe by
their Behaviour have given you fufficient Ground to infer, they
were carried away with fuch Objections So that they may be
able truly to deny the Objections ; and yet you think you can
prove them upon them, not from their *Words,* but from their
Behaviour. You will do well to give us fome Explication :
Suppofe you egregioufly miflook their Behaviour, and they
fay it had quite another Meaning In fhort, Sir, you are the
moft accomplifh'd Perfon in the Art of Shuffling I ever yet met
with : Firft you charge the Diffenting Teachers with teaching
falfe Doctrine, becaufe the People hold fuch and fuch Doctrines, and their Teachers do not go about to undeceive them;
and now the People are charg'd, not for their making thefe
falfe Doctrines their own Objections, but becaufe their holding
them may be infer'd from their Behaviour. Certainly this
kind of Evidence would not pafs in any Court, nor will it be
regarded by Men of Senfe. This does not look like the Difcourfe of a Man innocent in the Matter charg'd upon
him

You feem to lay a great Strefs on your Third Anfwer,
which has no manner of Strength in it.

You talk of your Letter to a Diffenting Parifhioner, with
which I was not in the leaft concern'd when I wrote my firft
Letter, having then never read it. And can it feem ftrange
to any Man, that your Parifhioners fhould never complain that
you had abus'd them, by publifhing thofe Eleven Inftances as
their Objections, when you do not pretend in that Letter to
have learn'd them of them ? This Pretence was ftarted in your
Examination, and no fooner did it appear, but it was complain'd of I never put the *Evafion* into their Heads, nor did I
any ways directly or indirectly move that an Enquiry fhould be
made · But after I had fent my Letter to the Prefs, that Information was fent me, That an Enquiry had been made, and that
fome of your Parifhioners on the reading of the 14*th* Page of your
Exa

Examination, had themselves taken notice of the Abuse · ʃ that I think this Matter is made sufficiently clear.

I confess, when I came to read *your Letter to a Dissenting Parishioner*, I could easily perceive that you father'd some ɑ your Objections therein on your Parishioners, and therefor when I was writing my Second Letter, I did desire a Friend ɩ enquire whether they own'd those Objections, and receiv'd a Answer, That they had mention'd some of them in Discourʃ with you, naming the Particulars And whatever Opinion ɑ thers may have of them, I look'd on the Answer as an Eviden they were plain, honest and well-meaning Men And I make n doubt, but they would have as freely own'd your Eleven In stances, as they did some of your Objections in *that Letter to Dissenting Parishioner*, if there had been as good Reason fo it.

So that you may now fee that *this Subject*, when rightly un derstood, *will afford no Matter for Ridicule* (unless you are dɪ pos'd to ridicule your felf) I can't but think you have Incli nation enough that way, your whole Management shews it but you want an Opportunity And tho I am not fond of ci ting Scraps of Latin, yet I fear not the Judgment of any impar tial Person, whether the exposing what is extreamly ridicu lous, as I did, is either *ped intul* or *foolish* Or whether even that way I took, was not (as I defign'd it) expressive of a juʃ neglect of what was fo excessively trifling

In your Fourth Answer, you tell me of some *Dissenters* (wh live not fo off) who say, that not ɩ u, but I, h ɩ misrepresɑ ɩ them, and ɩ displeas'd and down rɪght angry ɩ th me, for d owning thɑ ɩ Opinions, ɩ ɩ to be liked'd

For my part, I never pretended thɑ ɩ ll the Diss nters w of my mind, nɩ do I think it Prin ɑ, if fome of them shou'ɩ dislike fome things which I fay But I must confefs, it fɑɩ a little strange to me, that any of them should fay, *you ɩ not misrepresented them* I profefs I know no Dissenter, whe ther Presbyterian, Independent, or Anabaptist, who will fay fɑ of your first or last Instance And they can have no Reason to fay, that *I have misrepresented them*, who never pretended tɑ make any Representation of their Opinions at all, but only of fuch Opinions as were more generally held among the Dissen ters, and therefore I doubt not but upon Consideration, their Anger will be pacified, especially since I leave it most freelɑ to them to make what Representation they please of their own Opinion But this I can say, that my Representation hɑ been favourably receiv'd among all those differing Persuasion

fɑ

ſo far as I could ever hear, till you ſent me this Information.
And if I may be worthy to know what Corner thoſe Diſſenters
are in, I will give my ſelf the Trouble to enquire into the
Reaſons of their Diſpleaſure, that I may remove them   And
if it will be any means to engage you to give me ſuch a kind
Information, I will give you a ſomewhat like one concerning
the Reception of your Writings in this Town, and that is,
That whereas your Party were very confident in their Boaſtings
of your Performance as unanſwerable, before the Remarks appear'd, we hear now nothing of that nature, but they are as
ſilent in the Matter, as tho they were aſham'd of you, and ſome
of them have expreſly ſaid as much.

   Your laſt Conſideration is ſtrangely unaccountable, for
where as you charge thoſe Opinions on the common Diſſenters,
and then on their Teachers, Exam p 51   And at the End of
your Eleven Inſtances, ſay to Mr D   I ſet to Mr D p 21
Theſe, Sir, are the ſeveral Inſtances of falſe Doctrine ſpread a-
broad, and taught by the falſe Teachers of theſe Times, &c.
Tis plain you deſign'd to repreſent thoſe
Inſtances, as taught by the Diſſenters   ſee my 3d Let p 9.
And therefore if they are not taught by
them, you have miſrepreſented them.   And if your Teſtimonies are a Contradiction to this, I am not concern'd in the
Matter   It belongs to you, and not to me, to reconcile them
to your Letter

   And if there be any thing in that you ſay, why did you not
give up the Charge? Why did you ask me that Queſtion.
Fram Put I, if II   of   DI   Let
I as do of   I   I   I   I   if
us ſo m ſay, th   to   p n   the J   ſ
Approbation, is it le it   I   n

   And thus, Sir, I have anſwer it every trifling Letter   I
expect now, that without any more ado, you attempt a diſtinct
Anſwer to all my Letters, and a Vindication of all your   And
unleſs you do ſo, I muſt ſee better Reaſon than I can at preſent, to make me write any more   And had I not another
Anſwer to join with this, I ſhould never publiſh it   At leaſt
I delight not to impoſe upon the Reader with filling Paper
with needleſs Repetitions   Come therefore at length cloſe
to the Controverſy, and let me ſee that you are willing to
bring it to ſome Iſſue, (for tho I am willing to do any thing
that can be reaſonably deſir'd toward the clearing the Truth,
yet I abhor an endleſs and unprofitable Wrangling) And give
me occaſion to write an Anſwer of ſome juſt Size, and I will
                                                D   not

not (God willing) fail you: Or otherwife I now take leave you ; heartily thankful for the great Confirmation my Opin on has receiv'd by the means of your weak Oppofition , and I recommend you to the Divine Bleffing, wifhing you goc Health, and a found Judgment ;

And Remain,

Honoured Doctor,

Your moft Affectionate,

Newbury, *Feb*
the 12*th*, 170⁴

And Faithful Servant

In Chrift,

James Peirce.

Books *Printed for* J Lawrence, *at the* Angel *in the* Poultry

REmarks on Dr *Wells's* Letter to Mr *Peter Dowley* In Letter to a Friend The Second Edition 8o
Remarks on Dr *Wells's* Letter to a Diffenting Parifhioner In a Second Letter to a Friend The Second Edition 8o
A Defence of the Remarks on Dr *Wells's* Letter to Mr *Dowley* Being an Anfwer to the Firft and Second Parts of th Doctor's Examination In a Third and Fourth Letter 8o
A Continuation of the Defence of the Remarks on Dr *Wells's* Letters In a Fifth and Sixth Letter to the Doctor 8o. The Four by Mr *James Peirce*